# Developing Citiz

C000098193

## ACTIVITIES FOR PERSONAL, SOCIAL AND HEALTH EDUCATION

# year

## Christine Moorcroft

# A & C BLACK

# Contents

Published 2005 by A & C Black Publishers Limited
37 Soho Square, London W1D 3QZ
www.acblack.com

ISBN–10: 0-7136-7118-1
ISBN–13: 978-0-7136-7118-6

Editor: Jane Klima
Design: Susan McIntyre

*It Hurts* © John Foster 1997 from *Making Waves* (Oxford
University Press) included by permission of the author.

The author and publishers would like to thank Catherine Yemm
and Roy Honeybone for their assistance in producing this book.

A CIP catalogue record for this book is available from the
British Library.

Printed in Great Britain by St Edmundsbury Press,
Bury St Edmunds, Suffolk.

A & C Black uses paper produced with elemental chlorine-
free pulp, harvested from managed sustainable forests.

# Introduction

**Developing Citizenship** is a series of seven photocopiable activity books for citizenship lessons (including Personal, Social and Health Education and, in the foundation stage, *Personal, social and emotional development*). Each book provides a range of activities to help teachers to prepare children to play an active role as citizens, including:

- developing confidence and responsibility and making the most of their abilities;
- developing a healthy, safe lifestyle;
- developing good relationships and respecting differences between people;
- helping children to think for themselves, to express their own thoughts and opinions confidently, and to learn to listen to others' points of view;
- helping children to become full members of the groups they belong to, knowing they have rights but also becoming increasingly aware of their responsibilities.

The activities in **Year 2** are based on the QCA Scheme of Work for Citizenship at Key Stages 1 and 2 and support children's development in the following areas:

- understanding themselves as individuals and members of their communities;
- learning basic rules and skills for keeping themselves healthy and safe, and for behaving well;
- taking responsibility for themselves and their environment;
- understanding their own and other people's feelings;
- awareness of the views, needs and rights of other people;
- social skills such as taking turns, sharing, playing, helping others, resolving simple arguments and resisting bullying;
- participating in the life of their school and neighbourhood.

The activities are linked with other areas of the curriculum where appropriate and draw on the QCA schemes of work. Teachers are encouraged to create a stimulating classroom environment that provides opportunities for the children to develop a sense of responsibility: for example, they can keep the room tidy, organise equipment and write signs.

Each activity sheet features a **Teachers' note** at the foot of the page, which may be masked before photocopying. Expanded teaching notes are provided in **Notes on the activities** on pages 5–11. Most of the activity sheets end with a challenge (**Now try this!**) which reinforces and extends the children's learning and provides the teacher with an opportunity for assessment. These activities might be appropriate for only a few children; it is not expected that the whole class should complete them. A separate sheet of paper will be needed for some extension activities.

## Beyond the classroom

The series takes into account that unplanned experiences which the children have at school and in other places can contribute to the development of concepts and attitudes concerning citizenship. To help teachers to link children's learning through taught activities with their learning at other times, the teachers' notes make suggestions wherever possible for promoting the development of citizenship outside lesson times.

## Organisation

The activities require very few resources beyond pencils, scissors, card and other general classroom items. Any other materials you will need are specified in the **Notes on the activities** (for example, computers, information books and leaflets, pictures and story books).

## Reading

Most children will be able to carry out the activities independently. It is not expected that they should be able to read all the instructions on the sheets, but that someone will read them to or with them. Children gradually become accustomed to seeing instructions, and learn their purpose long before they can read them for themselves.

## Vocabulary

Key vocabulary to be introduced is provided in the **Notes on the activities**.

## Health and safety

**Developing Citizenship** provides advice on how to make lessons safe and how to encourage children to take responsibility for their own safety. Specific health and safety notes are included in the **Notes on the activities** where appropriate. Advice on implementing safe policy and practice for use of the Internet in schools can be found on the British Educational Communications and Technology Agency's website: www.becta.org.uk.

## Useful websites

**Citizenship education curriculum**: www.dfes.gov.uk/citizenship (summarises the citizenship curriculum, offers free resources for teachers, links to the QCA schemes of work)

**Institute for Citizenship**: www.citizen.org.uk/education (ideas for classroom activities; links to websites offering useful information)

**Schoolzone**: www.schoolzone.co.uk (resources for teaching citizenship)

**Eduwight** (Isle of Wight Council's website for children's services): http://eduwight.iow.gov.uk/curriculum/vocational/citizenship/ (resources for teaching citizenship, including lesson plans)

**PSHE and citizenship links**: www.jamesbancrofteducation.net/pshe (online resources, including assembly ideas, for various citizenship topics, such as bullying; links to children's websites, including Childline and Kidscape)

**Kelly Bear** (a U.S. website featuring a positive role model for children aged 3–9): www.kellybear.com/TeacherArticles/TeacherTip27.html (20 ideas for teaching citizenship, including lesson plans)

The notes in this section expand upon those provided at the foot of each activity sheet. They give ideas for making the most of the sheet, including suggestions for a whole-class introduction, the plenary session or for follow-up work using an adapted version of the page.

The notes also suggest links which can be made with other areas of the curriculum and ways of developing citizenship through everyday experiences: for example, involving the children in the planning of school events, discussing any problems the school faces and their possible solutions, and involving the children in planning for changes at the school. An example faced by one school was the amalgamation with a neighbouring school. The teachers asked the children to think of ways of welcoming the newcomers and helping them to settle in.

To help teachers to select appropriate learning experiences for their pupils, the activities are grouped into sections within each book, but the pages need not be presented in the order in which they appear, unless stated otherwise.

Where appropriate, stories, songs, rhymes, jingles and poems are suggested for introducing the activities or rounding them off.

## Taking part

These activities develop skills of communication, participation in decision-making activities and contribution to school life. They build on work from **Year 1**. The children also have opportunities to contribute to discussions.

**Tuning in** (page 12) develops the children's understanding of what is involved in effective listening by encouraging them to think about what they do when they listen to one another. Ask them what they do when they are told to listen in class (for example, sit up, stop talking, face the person speaking). Then enact a short conversation with another adult in which you demonstrate poor listening: for example, looking out of the window when the other is talking, filing your nails and admiring them, turning away from the speaker, leafing through a book or magazine, yawning, playing with things such as tiddlywinks (or anything which will amuse the children). You could even enact some of the things the children do when they are not listening properly in class. Ask the children if they think you were listening. Why not? List their observations and ask them what you should have done. Higher-attaining children could write some instructions for being a good listener. They could also discuss what makes a good speaker (so that people *want* to listen). Link this with literacy (writing instructions).

**Vocabulary:** *ask, face, listen, look, question, speak, talk.*

**Chat** (page 13) develops the children's ability to respond to others. It builds on the listening skills developed in **Tuning in**, page 12. Encourage them to ask their partner questions and challenge them to find out as much as possible about their partner's hobbies (for example, where they carry out the activity and what they use) before swapping roles to tell their partners about *their* hobbies. Set a timer, such as a sand timer, to limit the time each one of the pair talks; they swap over when the timer stops. You could model this by telling the children what you have found out about another adult's hobby. Instead of writing their responses, lower-attaining children could tell an adult what they have found out about their partner's hobby. Link this with geography (the places the children visit, drawing simple maps and how they spend their time) and with literacy (asking and answering questions and punctuating sentences and questions).

**Vocabulary:** *ask, hobby, listen, partner, question, speak, talk, tell.*

**The red robot** and **Red robot rules** (pages 14–15) develop skills of discussion and co-operation in a group and provide an opportunity for the children to take part in setting ground rules. Begin by reminding them of situations at school in which everyone wants to play with the same toy or to use the same piece of equipment. What should they do if the same person always seems to be using it? Help them to think up a system in which they can take turns: for example, a rota which they tick after each session in which they have used this toy or equipment. What have they learned from the story? This could be linked with literacy (writing rules and instructions and writing stories in chronological order).

**Vocabulary:** *fair, instructions, rules, share, turn, wait.*

**Have your say** (page 16) develops the children's ability to take part in a discussion and to take account of different views. Point out that there are  some issues where most people agree what is right and what is wrong but that people have different likes and dislikes; these are neither right nor wrong. Also make it clear that the children are not being asked to comment on one another's behaviour at playtime – this is not a 'tale-telling' session. You could link this with literacy by introducing it through poems about everyday issues such as playtime or likes and dislikes: for example, *Our side of the playground* by Judith Nicholls (from *Playtime Poems*, collected by Jill Bennett, OUP), *Boys and girls come out to play* (traditional, in *The Oxford Nursery Rhyme Book*, Iona & Peter Opie, OUP) or *First and last* by June Crebbin (in *The Puffin Book of Fantastic First Poems*, edited by June Crebbin, OUP).

**Vocabulary:** *bad, chat, discussion, dislike, good, like, play.*

**For or against** (page 17) encourages the children to express an opinion about a real-life issue and to recognise that there can be conflicting views. Remind them that they should take turns to speak and should listen to one another during discussions. Link this with work on animals in science lessons, when they are encouraged to look after any animals they study and to return them to where they found them. Ask them if everyone should look after all animals (remind them that 'animals' include insects and animals that some people are scared of, such as rats and snakes). Point out that people buy equipment and chemicals designed to kill some animals that they consider to be pests. Ask the children which animals some people think are pests, and why. Discuss what Mrs Lee could do instead of killing the flies in her kitchen. She might not want to close the window if the kitchen is hot or steamy. Point out that there are products which are designed to keep flies away rather than killing them. Let the children make up their own minds about what is the right answer. Higher-attaining children might be able to present a simple argument for or against killing flies in the kitchen.

> **Vocabulary:** *against, animal, care, for, insect, kill.*

**Pick and choose** (page 18) develops the children's ability to recognise that there can be conflicting views and that they may need to compromise when making a decision. Ask them what children sometimes do when the others do not agree with their choice. Draw out that there are times when everyone has to compromise. Introduce the words *compromise* and *negotiate* and explain what they mean. Draw out the importance of learning how to agree and disagree and how to negotiate an outcome that both sides accept. Introduce or revise writing instructions (link this with literacy) for the children who tackle the extension activity.

> **Vocabulary:** *agree, compromise, different, disagree, fair, listen, negotiate, unfair.*

**Helping Hannah: 1** and **2** (pages 19–20) are about recognising the choices which can be made in solving problems. The children should first have had opportunities to discuss the meaning of bullying. Draw out that, as well as physical harm, it includes any actions or words which hurt, upset or frighten people on a sustained basis. Some children could also read some of the advice (or the teacher could select items to read with them) on websites such as:
>     www.kidscape.org.uk
>     www.dfes.gov.uk/bullying/pupilindex
>     www.bbc.co.uk/schools/bullying
>     www.antibully. org.uk
>     http://hometown.aol.co.uk/ellelouiselang/bullying. html
Link this with work in literacy (letter-writing): the children could also write a letter from Hannah, asking a friend to help her.

> **Vocabulary:** *advice, bully, bullying, choice, frighten, harm, hurt, sustained, upset.*

# Choices

This section provides opportunities for the children to discuss what they like and dislike and what is right and what is wrong; they develop skills in decision-making. The activities also include the choice which can be made about lifestyles; the children develop an understanding of the choices they make which can affect their health, well-being and safety. The activities build on similar work from **Year 1**.

**Two wrongs ...** (page 21) develops the children's understanding of the difference between right and wrong. Discuss what they should do or say if they accidentally hurt or bump into someone. Draw out that if that person acts in an angry way it is not so easy to say they are sorry, but that they should still do so – introduce the saying 'Two wrongs do not make a right'. This could be linked with literacy (using *because* to link ideas in sentences). Use this activity in connection with real incidents at school, when

children turn on someone who has hurt them by accident. Discuss the consequences of this. The other person is likely to become angry too, even if he or she was going to apologise.

> **Vocabulary:** *accident, accidental, accidentally, angry, apologise, because, deliberate, harm, hurt, sorry, upset.*

**Right and wrongs** (page 22) helps to develop the children's understanding of the difference between right and wrong by focusing on behaviour which is safe or dangerous, responsible or irresponsible, friendly or unfriendly and considerate or inconsiderate (although not all of these terms need to be introduced at this stage). Discuss what makes some actions wrong: they harm other people, animals or property or upset or frighten people or animals. Draw out that the children can make choices about how they behave. Which people in the picture have made the wrong choices (and which ones have made the right choices)? Higher-attaining children could write short recounts about what might happen next in the picture. You could link this with literacy.

> **Vocabulary:** *bad, care, dangerous, friendly, good, harm, hurt, right, safe, unfriendly, unsafe, wrong.*

**Goody bag** (page 23) develops the children's understanding of the meanings of the words *fair* and *unfair*. They could begin by sharing real objects among their group. What do they do if anything is left over? Can it be split up or can they take turns to use it? If not, what can they do? They might suggest drawing lots (or a method with a similar chance element) or giving the left-over item to the teacher. Are they all satisfied that the outcome was fair? Ask them what *fair* means. Draw out that it means treating everyone equally. They could draw a picture of the outcome of their sharing the goody bag. During circle time the children could talk about times when they feel unfairly treated: for example, their older brother or sister can stay up later than them or can watch programmes they are not allowed to see. Help them to understand that some of these situations are fair, and to reason why. Higher-attaining children could add an explanation of why the outcome of this page was fair. This could be linked with work in maths on division and remainders.

> **Vocabulary:** *divide, equal, fair, same, share, unfair.*

**Pirates' shopping list** (page 24) helps the children to recognise the choices they can make in connection with what they eat. Discuss the times when they can choose what they eat. What do they choose? Point out that that we should eat more of some foods than others because they contain ingredients we need to stay healthy: for example, fruit and vegetables. Can the children think of any fruits and vegetables which the ship's stores do not have in stock? Also point out that we should eat less of some foods than others because they contain a lot of fat or sugar. Explain that too much fat can make us overweight and that too much sugar can harm our teeth. Ask the children how they can tell which foods are sugary or fatty (they taste sweet or they have a greasy feel). You could also read the ingredients on food labels with some children.

> **Vocabulary:** *choice, choose, fat, food, fruit, healthy, sugar, vegetables.*

**Give germs the boot!** (page 25) focuses on the choices the children can make about food hygiene. You could show them magnified photographs of germs on surfaces, food and skin and explain that these are tiny living things we cannot see. Point out that there are also many tiny living things that do not do us any harm  and even some that are helpful. It might be appropriate to introduce the term *micro-organism* for tiny living things and to explain that we use the word *germ* for micro-organisms that can harm us. Tell the children about some of the harm that germs can do: for example, causing illnesses such as stomach upsets or coughs and colds, which might then be passed on to other people. Explain that washing removes many germs and that heat kills germs. If necessary, ask lower-attaining children to describe what they see in the pictures, then ask them to tell you what you should do. Then help them to write their instructions. This can be linked with work in literacy (writing instructions).

> **Vocabulary:** *food, germ, heat, illness, wash, wipe.*

**Magic lamp** (page 26) encourages the children to share their opinions on matters which are important to them. It could be introduced by reading a simplified version of the story of Aladdin from the Arabian Nights (for example, *Disney Classics: Aladdin*, Ladybird). Discuss Aladdin's wishes (he asked only for what he and his mother needed and for what he had been promised – the princess for a wife). Ask the children to think of anything important they would like to change. Discuss whom it would help, and how, and the idea of unselfish wishes. The children could make one wish for themselves and two for other people. This could be linked with RE. They might be able to write their own 'magic lamp' stories. You could discuss the consequences of the children's wishes. What might happen that was not in the original wish?

> **Vocabulary:** *change, help, important, issue, opinion, selfish, unselfish, wish.*

**The right answer** (page 27) helps the children to appreciate the influences that can affect the choices they make. It deals with helpful and unhelpful behaviour, anti-social behaviour and substance abuse. Any of these topics could be developed during other lessons. During the plenary session, ask the children how they answered the questions. Ask them to explain their answers. The following websites provide activities for children in connection with substance abuse:

http://homepage.virgin.net/ride.drugeducation
www.darekids.co.uk

> **Vocabulary:** *bad, behaviour, choice, different, good, refuse, right, wrong.*

**William's guinea pig** (page 28) helps the children to learn about rights and responsibilities when making decisions. It can be linked with work in literacy and science (the needs of animals) and is based on *William and the Guinea Pig* (Thinkers series, Gill Rose & Tim Archbold, A & C Black): William asks his mother if he can have a guinea pig, promising that he will take care of it. His younger sister, Kelly, shares his excitement when he is given a guinea pig for his birthday; she asks if she can help but he says 'No, you are too young', and refuses to let her touch the guinea pig. Kelly creeps into the shed where the guinea pig's hutch is kept and plays with it from time to time. After a while William begins to neglect the guinea pig, until his cousin arrives one day and his mother suggests that he show her the guinea

pig. William suddenly remembers that he has neither fed it nor cleaned its hutch for a long time and is scared that it might be ill or even dead. To his surprise the guinea pig is clean, well-fed and healthy (Kelly has been looking after it). Kelly doesn't tell their mother what she has been doing. Discuss whose behaviour was responsible and whose was not, how William feels and how Kelly feels. What good did Kelly's responsible behaviour do? In addition to keeping the guinea pig healthy and happy, in what other way did Kelly help William? Discuss what made William make the wrong choice (he wanted to play football with his friend and kept putting off cleaning and feeding the guinea pig). Some children might be able to write notes about the story and re-tell it in their own words.

> **Vocabulary:** *choice, clean, feed, food, help, need, responsibility, responsible, shelter, water.*

**Copycat** (page 29) helps the children to understand that the pressure to behave in an unacceptable way can come from people they know and to learn how to resist pressure to act in a way they know is wrong. Discuss the choices the children in the examples can make. What are the right choices? What might lead them to make the wrong choices? Encourage the children to recognise the times when they can make a choice and to bring to mind what they know about right and wrong. Ensure that the children know why building sites are dangerous (machinery which can topple over, sharp items, holes in the ground and harmful materials). The following websites provide children's activities and information connected with building sites:

www.splaat.com
www.buildingsitesbite.co.uk

> **Vocabulary:** *bad, building site, choice, danger, dangerous, good, right, safe, safety, unsafe, wrong.*

**Come and buy** (page 30) develops the children's understanding of the effects of advertisements. Discuss how sometimes people who are content with what they have see advertisements and begin to want other things and even to believe that they need those things. Draw out why the children cannot always have what they want (there are limits to what their parents can spend and to what they want to spend on toys and non-essential items). Also encourage the children to think of children who have no toys. They might want to contribute to schemes for sending gifts to needy children. This activity could be linked with maths (money) and literacy (rhymes and jingles).

> **Vocabulary:** *advertisement, cost, need, new, want.*

## Animals and us

The activities in this section develop the idea of rights and responsibilities. They focus on the needs of humans and other animals and have a strong link with science. They also explore animal welfare and the responsibilities of humans towards animals and could be developed through contact with local branches of animal welfare organisations such as the RSPCA (www.rspca.org.uk) and PDSA (www.pdsa.org.uk).

**Needs** (page 31) is about the needs all humans have: for air, food, water and shelter. In order to be healthy, they also need exercise. Draw out that people cannot survive without air, water, food and shelter and, although they can survive without friendship, love and affection, most people need these in order to be happy. This can be linked with work in science (Ourselves).

> **Vocabulary:** *air, breathe, clothes, drink, eat, exercise, fit, food, home, shelter, water, wear.*

**Animal match: 1, 2** and **3** (pages 32–34) help the children to learn about the needs of animals. They will need access to information books, CDs or the Internet to find out about the animals featured on these pages. The children could take the role of an animal and 'introduce themselves' to their group who have to guess which animal they are (from those depicted).

Answers:

| Animal | Favourite foods | Favourite places | Greatest fears | Why I am important |
|---|---|---|---|---|
| Crow | grain, berries, insects, dead animals, other birds' eggs | farmland | farmers, game-keepers | I get rid of dead animals and insects which harm crops. |
| Fox | birds, other small animals | farmland, woods and gardens | hunters, dogs | I get rid of pests such as mice and rats. |
| Greenfly | the sap of plants | leaves | ladybirds, other beetles, small birds, garden sprays | I am a good food for garden birds. |
| Hedgehog | slugs, insects | piles of leaves | bonfires | I eat animals which harm garden plants and crops. |
| Mouse | grain, fruit, insects, biscuits | buildings | cats, foxes, owls | Foxes eat me instead of killing hens. |
| Snail | living and dead plants | gardens | gardeners, thrushes, slug pellets | I get rid of dead plants in the garden. |
| Spider | flies, other small insects | gardens, buildings | large birds | I eat flies and other insect pests. |
| Thrush | snails | gardens | sparrow hawks | I eat snails and slugs, which damage plants. |

Discuss why some people dislike these animals or consider them to be pests. What harm do they do?

> **Vocabulary:** *beetle, bonfire, crops, crow, farmer, flies, fox, game-keeper, garden spray, grain, greenfly, hedgehog, hunter, ladybird, mouse, owl, pest, plants, sap, slug, slug pellet, snail, sparrow hawk, spider, thrush.*

**Wildlife garden** (page 35) is about the responsibility humans have for animals. It could be linked with the development or management of a school wildlife garden in connection with work in science and geography. The children could word-process the text for interpretive panels for a wildlife garden. See also:
 www.english-nature.org.uk/science/nature_for_schools
 www.goring-by-sea.uk.com/palatine
 www.hants.gov.uk/schoolgardens
 www.ngs.org.uk/yellow_book
 www.bgci.org.uk/education/outdoor_ classroom
Find out more about wildlife-friendly gardening from:
 www.bbc.co.uk/nature/animals/wildbritain/makespace

> **Vocabulary:** *danger, endangered, protect, wildlife.*

# People who help us – the local police

These activities are about the work of the police and would be enhanced through contact with the local police station or a visit from their schools liaison officer. The activities develop the children's awareness of the work of the police and provide opportunities to explore issues of identity and responsibility. The children also learn what is meant by *emergency* and how to deal with emergencies.

**On the beat** (page 36) is about the basic roles of the police, including crime prevention and detection, public protection, law and order in public places and public safety. Do the children know the meaning of *beat* in this context? You will probably need to explain it. Invite the children to take turns to say what they think of when the word *police* is mentioned: for example, arrest, criminal, fine, help. Their knowledge of the police could come from a variety of sources, including television (fiction and news), visits to police stations and contact with individual police officers. Ask them what they have seen police officers doing and why they do it. Draw out that their role is to keep people, places and property safe. Focus on some of the ways in which they do this: showing and telling people how to take care of themselves and their property, stopping people who harm property, animals and other people or who act in a way that could cause harm (for example, by driving too fast or throwing stones or other objects in public places), arresting people, and so on (see www.police.uk).

> **Vocabulary:** *arrest, beat, constable, crime, danger, fine, help, officer, police, robbery, safe, safety, uniform, warn.*

**Missing** and **Keep it safe** (pages 37–38) develop the children's understanding of individual and collective responsibilities. They focus on responsibilities at school. Introduce or revise the word *responsibility* and ask the children for examples. Focus on responsibility for property and draw out that the children should be able to look after their own property rather than relying on adults to do it for them. Ask them what might have happened to the lost jumper: Tal could have forgotten where he left it, left it somewhere where it could be kicked out of sight or picked up by someone else by mistake, someone might have taken it thinking it was theirs or it could have been stolen or hidden by someone. Discuss how these mishaps can be prevented at school, including ensuring that their property is labelled with their name. You could also discuss what should happen to lost property at school that no one claims. Ask the children for suggestions, encourage them to choose the best suggestion and help them to put it into practice. Link this with literacy by asking the children to write instructions for looking after their property or signs or lists for a lost property cupboard. You could also read *Joe Giant's Missing Boot* by Toni Goffe (Walker Books); the children could write a story about the adventures of a lost shoe.

> **Vocabulary:** *forget, forgotten, hidden, label, lose, lost, missing, mistake, property, responsibility, steal, stole, stolen, take, took.*

**Emergency call**, **Help!** and **Hoax** (pages 39–41) are about what to do in an emergency, about how to decide if a mishap is an emergency and about the consequences of making hoax 999 calls. Through practising what to do if they ever have to make an emergency call, the children are likely to remember the procedure. Point out that they might want to start telling the operator about the problem immediately but that they will first have to give details such as their phone number, name and address. The children could enact the procedure in groups, using different services: ambulance, police, fire brigade and coastguard. Help them to describe their location effectively (link this with work in geography) and, where necessary, provide practice in writing their addresses and phone numbers. Point out that an emergency is when there is danger to people or if a serious crime is witnessed and the police could arrive in time to catch the culprit, such as someone breaking into a house or car. You might be able to arrange a visit from a representative of one of the emergency services to inform the children what happens *after* an emergency call has been placed. Introduce and explain the word *hoax*. Ask the children what a hoax 999 call is. Discuss why some people make hoax calls and make clear that all our actions have consequences. After the children have completed page 41, draw out that, even if the children in the story were making the call for fun and did not mean to harm anyone, they should have thought about the consequences of what they were doing: if a fire engine and its crew were sent to a place where they were not needed they could not be ready for a real emergency. BT's website provides information about campaigns to stop children making hoax 999 calls: www.payphones.bt.com/2001/about/hoax_calls. Higher-attaining children might be able to write a play-script based on an emergency.

> **Vocabulary:** *address, ambulance, coastguard, consequences, crime, emergency services, fire brigade, harm, harmful, help, hoax, phone number, police.*

**On the safe side** (page 42) develops the children's skills in keeping themselves safe. Although adults are responsible for children's safety, children can take responsibility for some aspects of this and gradually increase their responsibility as they become capable. Different children are allowed different amounts of freedom to go out alone. Some might be allowed to play in parks alone, but even those who go there with adults need to be aware of the safety issues connected with water, animals, high places and people who might want to harm them. Ask them to point out the possible dangers in the picture.

> **Vocabulary:** *bite, dangerous, drown, fall, high, safe, stranger.*

**A question of trust** (page 43) is about individual and collective responsibilities in relation to personal safety; it helps the children to recognise whom they can trust. Point out that most people do not want to harm children but that it is difficult to know which people to trust. How can the children be sure whom to trust? Draw out that it is safe to speak to police officers and people in certain jobs in the community. They can identify police officers by their uniforms and they can identify people whose jobs involve talking to children and other people in the community: for example, crossing patrol helpers, shop assistants, librarians, dentists, doctors. They can recognise people who are known to their families. Tell the children that if anyone, even someone they know and thought they could trust, does anything which upsets them, they should point this out by telling another trusted adult. This activity can be linked with work in literacy on reported speech and writing questions.

> **Vocabulary:** *danger, safe, safety, stranger, trust.*

**Safety in numbers** (page 44) helps the children to develop strategies for keeping themselves safe. They should recognise that May avoids secluded places, such as the woods. She walks on, ignoring the man she does not know who says hello to her. She crosses the road (on a crossing) to see if he does the same, going towards a place where there are plenty of people (shops). He is still following as she leaves the shops, but later he has stopped. Why did he stop following her? Perhaps it was coincidence – he had just been going the same way, or maybe May stopped and spoke to someone or knocked at the door of a house. Tell the children that if anyone they do not know speaks to them when they are alone, it is not bad manners to ignore them and walk on. If they think the person is following them, they could check by crossing the road in a safe place and see if the person is still following, but they should head in the direction of a place such as a shop or house, where there are other people, and even go into a shop or knock on a door or ring a doorbell. See also www.green-park.co.uk for children's activities in connection with personal safety. After the children have completed the activity, invite volunteers to say what May does at one of the question marks, and why.

> **Vocabulary:** *busy, danger, dangerous, quiet, route, safe, safety.*

**Presents** (page 45) focuses on one way in which people might try to bribe children. Draw out that most presents are given for good reasons but some are known as bribes. Stress that most people do not want to harm children but that if anyone they do not know offers them anything or asks if they would like to go anywhere, they should get away from this person immediately. They might ask what to do if someone tries to get hold of them. They should shout and yell as loudly as they can; help them to practise shouting from the stomach (rather than from the throat). Discuss what they could shout: for example, 'Help!'

**Vocabulary:** *alone, bribe, help, present.*

# Living in a diverse world

In these activities the children learn about identities and communities. The activities introduce basic human needs and rights and equality among people. They develop the children's understanding of respect for themselves and others, membership of communities (including school and family) and about the differences and similarities between people.

**All kinds of people: 1** and **2** (pages 46–47) focus on recognising and showing respect for similarities and differences. The children are likely to find various ways of sorting the pictures; discuss the similarities that all people have and then the differences  the children have spotted. Ask them about the ways in which the people in one set are similar; how are they different from the others? How are they similar to people in other sets? Discuss other ways in which they have sorted the pictures. Ask them if it would be fair to group people at school in these ways.

**Vocabulary:** *age, difference, different, disability, gender, race, same, similar, similarity.*

 **School visitors, Interview** and **Out and about** (pages 48–50) are about the people the children meet in their school and local community. Encourage them to find out about these people and to take an interest in them. Ask them to name any visitors they know who come to the school. When do they come, and why? If the school has a visitors' book, you could read some of the entries with the children. Also make them aware of any systems the school has for monitoring visitors and for security. Do visitors wear special badges when they are in or around the building? Do they sign the visitors' book when they arrive and leave? Discuss how the children can identify visitors who are meant to be in the school. After the interview, invite feedback from the children. They could contribute to a class display about people who visit the school; include photographs of the visitors and any information they want to give: for example, about their families, pets, homes, and so on. Some children could tape-record the interviews and then write reports based on their recordings. Link this with literacy.

**Vocabulary:** *answer, interview, local community, question, security, visitor.*

**Home sweet home** (page 51) develops the children's understanding of, and respect for, diversity in communities. For this activity it is useful to set up links with another school in a different cultural setting, using e-mail. Before beginning this page, the children could carry out a homework activity to make notes about the information they will need. Draw out that people have different kinds of homes and furnish them differently, depending on their lifestyles. If the school has travelling families they might be able to arrange a visit to the site so that the others can find out about mobile homes, including the places they visit. This could be linked with map work in geography.

**Vocabulary:** *drawing room, furniture, home, living room, lounge, sitting room.*

**Monster train** (page 52) uses monsters to help the children to recognise diversity and to focus on equality among people. Ask them if it is fair that some monsters can travel in the best carriages but others are not allowed to. Would it be all right if they were allowed to travel in any carriage but had to pay more in the better ones? What do they think the cheapest ones should be like? Explain that the very first trains had open carriages with no roofs and that people who travelled in them paid low fares but sometimes got very cold and wet (there were even reports of people becoming seriously ill or dying after such journeys); open carriages were banned and now there are different types of carriage but the cheaper ones are comfortable. The issue in this activity is of some people being barred from places. Tell the children that this has happened until very recently in some places: for example, black and white children attending separate schools in southern states of the USA and in South Africa. You could introduce the terms *racism* and *racist* and discuss what they mean.

**Vocabulary:** *different, fair, racism, racist, similar, unfair.*

**Fair for all, Aliens all** and **Hurting** (pages 53–55) help the children to realise that all human beings have the same basic rights, to develop strategies to deal with prejudice and to show support for others who encounter prejudice. Discuss the idea of equal opportunities (this term could be introduced if appropriate) and whether it means treating everyone in exactly the same way. The children should notice which differences are  fair and which are unfair: for example, it is considered fair to charge children lower fares than adults on public transport but not to treat men and women or boys and girls differently. Ask the children if it is fair to keep some seats for people with disabilities; establish that some people might need different types of help to enable them to do the same things as other people. Note that people sometimes avoid others who are different from themselves in some way, but point out that there are more similarities than differences.

**Vocabulary:** *age, disability, gender, hostile, prejudice, race, racism.*

**Bullying** and **Beat the bullies** (pages 56–57) give the children an opportunity to work in pairs to share their views about an issue which affects all schools. Page 56 focuses on the meaning of bullying and invites the children to give examples of behaviour which is classed as bullying. Discuss what distinguishes bullying from other kinds of behaviour: it harms, upsets or frightens other people and includes hitting, kicking or other physical harm, name-calling, pulling faces and making unpleasant remarks. Emphasise that bullying is a sustained activity, not just a one-off incident. Page 57 deals with strategies for coping with bullying. Draw out that it is important to report bullying because anyone who bullies others will not want to be found out. Also introduce strategies such as avoiding being alone in places where you could be bullied and ignoring comments made by bullies. See also:

www.kidscape.org.uk
www.bullying.co.uk
www.dfes.gov.uk/index

> **Vocabulary:** *bully, bullying, frighten, harm, hurt, scare, sustained, upset.*

## Developing our school grounds

This section involves the children in observation, discussion, problem-solving and co-operation. It introduces them to working in a democratic way which takes into consideration the needs and wishes of the whole community. It can be linked with work in geography on the use of maps and plans.

**A place to sit**, **Playground features**, **Playground survey** and **Our choice** (pages 58–61) give the children an opportunity to reflect on what they like and dislike, to discuss issues and to consult with the school community, working in groups. Ask them to imagine they are in this playground. What could they do there? What might be difficult? What makes it a comfortable and pleasant place? Is there anything which spoils its appearance and comfort? This could be linked with work on safety in the sun. In an ICT lesson, you could set up an e-mail link with another school in a different setting (for example, urban or rural, a different part of the country or abroad) and exchange digital photographs of one another's playgrounds. Display these photographs and ask the children to name the features they can see. Which features do they like, and why? Which do they have in their own playground? Which would they like? This work could also be linked with art: the children could draw sketches of their own playground. Point out that it is not always possible to put the children's ideas into practice because of the time or cost, but that when there is a budget for playground improvements, the children's ideas can be considered.

> **Vocabulary:** *comfortable, garden, litter, plants, playground, pleasant, safe, seats, shade, shelter, trees.*

**Finding out** (page 62) provides an opportunity to consult others in the school community and to work in groups on an issue of interest to them all. Ask them to think about how they use the school playground. What do they do at playtimes? Help them to categorise the activities according to type, as shown on the chart. Do they have any problems when carrying out any of these activities? Invite them to talk about problems: for example, bumping into one another, being knocked over, not having enough space. Link this with literacy: the children could collaborate on writing a non-chronological report about activities in the playground.

> **Vocabulary:** *chat, community, movement, play, playground, problem, suitable, unsuitable.*

**Suggestions box** (page 63) develops the children's ability to consult one another and to generate and explore ideas; it provides a format on which they can record their comments about a shared issue. Provide a box into which they can place their  completed suggestions forms and encourage them to discuss the suggestions made by the class; remind them that they should take turns during a discussion and listen to the person speaking. They could select the suggestions they think could be carried out, and explain why – and why the others could not be carried out (or why this might be difficult). Help them to select a suggestion on which the class could act (see **Agreeing and disagreeing**, page 64). Issues could be addressed through the school council, if it has one. If not, you could consider setting one up (see www.schoolcouncils.org).

> **Vocabulary:** *agree, disagree, discuss, listen, suggest, suggestion, take turns.*

**Agreeing and disagreeing** (page 64) develops the children's understanding about the importance of consultation. They should realise that all views are valid and that sometimes they will disagree with one another, but they can still agree on a course of action which is decided by most of them (you could introduce the term *majority*). Draw out that if they listen to other ideas they might be convinced by them and change their opinion. They could use a simple voting system as shown in the extension activity. Another extension could be to find the views of a different class for comparison.

> **Vocabulary:** *agree, disagree, discuss, majority, most, opinion, vote.*

# Tuning in

## Are they good listeners? ✔ or ✗

### • Explain your answers.

I went to the park on Sunday.

I like those trainers. Do you?

Yes. They're cool.

Shareen – guess where I've been for my holiday. Jamaica!

I'm getting good at this.

Now try this!

• **Write three things a good listener does.**
• **Write three things a good speaker does.**

**Teachers' note** Ask the children how they can tell if someone is not listening to the person speaking. Draw out that they might turn away from the speaker, look at other people or objects around them, fidget, chat or play games. How can they tell if people are listening? Establish that they face the speaker, look at the speaker, look interested, say something about the subject the speaker talked about and ask questions.

**Developing Citizenship**
**Year 2**
© A & C BLACK

# Chat

- **Work with a partner.**
- **Chat about one of his or her hobbies.**
- **Write some notes.**

Listen.
Ask questions.

My partner's hobby

_____

_____

_____

Where my partner does this

_____

_____

_____

Things my partner uses

_____

_____

_____

Now try this!

**What does your partner like about this hobby?**

_____

_____

**Teachers' note** The children should first listen to a partner telling them about his or her hobby. Allow up to five minutes for this (use a sand timer) and then ask the children to swap roles and after that to complete the page about their partner's hobby. The extension activity encourages them to ask their partner questions.

Developing Citizenship
**Year 2**
© A & C BLACK

# The red robot

- **Read the story with your group.**
- **Talk about what went wrong.**

Everyone liked the red robot.

I want the red robot.

Max always got it first.

One day Ella took the robot from Max.

Max snatched it back.

There was a fight. The robot was broken.

No one can play with it now.

 Now try this!

- **Make the story happy.**
- **Draw and write your story.**

**Teachers' note** After the children have read the story, ask them what caused the problem. What was unfair? Discuss why Ella acted as she did. Was this the best way to deal with something unfair? Discuss what else she could have done and how this would have led to a happy ending.

**Developing Citizenship
Year 2**
© **A & C BLACK**

- **Write three rules for playing with the red robot.**

1 _____

_____

_____

2 _____

_____

_____

3 _____

_____

Now try this!

- **Use a computer to key in all your group's rules.**

**Teachers' note** Ask the children how rules could have helped the children in the story of the red robot on page 14. Discuss what rules are for and draw out that it is easier to obey rules if there are not too many of them. How might these three rules have helped the children in the story?

**Developing Citizenship**
**Year 2**
© A & C BLACK

15

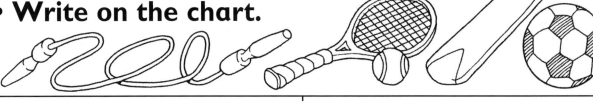

## What do you think about playtime?

• **Write on the chart.**

| What is good? | What is not good? |
|---|---|
| | |

• **Choose one thing from the second list.**
• **Write how you would change it.**
• **Draw a picture.**

**Teachers' note** The children should first have the opportunity to discuss playtime and to think about what they like and what they dislike about it and to consider the reasons. For some children this will be an opportunity to talk about problems at playtime.

**Developing Citizenship**
**Year 2**
© A & C BLACK

# For or against

- ## Work with a group.

## Should Mrs Lee kill the flies?

- ## Write your names on the chart.

| yes | no |
| --- | --- |
|  |  |
|  |  |
|  |  |
|  |  |

## What does your group think? _____

- ## Write a sentence about why you said yes or no .

**Teachers' note** Remind the children of how animals are cared for at school (for example, for work in science). What do they do with any animals brought in from outdoors? Draw out that they are responsible for providing the animals with what they need to stay alive and be comfortable. Ask them about unwanted animals which come into school, such as wasps, bees and flies. What should be done about them? Discuss why people buy fly-swatters and insect sprays.

**Developing Citizenship**
**Year 2**
© **A & C BLACK**

# Pick and choose

## What should these children do?

- **Talk to your group.**
- **Write your group's answer.**

_____

_____

_____

**Your group does not agree about where to sit at lunchtime.**

**What can you do?**

- **Write instructions.**

**Teachers' note** Ask the children what they think will happen in the picture. How should those children decide what to play? If the group decides to play 'Snap' who will be happy? How might the others feel? Draw out that when fair decisions are made some people might not like them. Only one copy of this page is needed for a group of children.

**Developing Citizenship
Year 2**
**© A & C BLACK**

- ## Work with a group.
  ## What can Hannah do?

No one is going to play with you.

Hannah

We'll get you at playtime.

- ## Write your group's answers in the speech bubbles.

**Teachers' note** Ask the children what is happening in the picture and how Hannah feels. Ask one child to act as scribe for the group; after they have discussed what she could do, invite feedback. Stress that no one should be bullied and that anyone who is bullied must tell a parent, teacher or other trusted adult and that they should never be afraid to do so.

**Developing Citizenship**
**Year 2**
© A & C BLACK

# Helping Hannah: 2

- **Write a letter to Hannah.**
- **Help her to feel better.**
- **Tell her what she could do.**

Dear Hannah

You must feel _____

_____

You could _____

_____

_____

_____

_____

_____

I hope_____

With best wishes

from _____

**Teachers' note** Discuss what might make it difficult for Hannah to take action to stop the bullying on page 19: for example, she might be afraid to tell anyone in case it led to more bullying. Who could help her, and how?

**Developing Citizenship**
**Year 2**
© A & C BLACK

# Two wrongs ...

**How do these children feel?**

**What should they do or say?**

- **Act out the stories with a partner.**

- **Change the stories.**
- **Make the children do** `right` .
- **Draw the new endings.**

**Teachers' note** Discuss how the children can enact the stories without hurting anyone. Stress that they should not bump into one another, spill water, and so on. Encourage them to try to remember times when someone has bumped into them, spilt things on their property or harmed them in some other way by accident. How did they feel? What did they do or say? Discuss the choices they can make about responding to accidental harm.

**Developing Citizenship Year 2**
**© A & C BLACK**

# Rights and wrongs

- **Colour red anyone who is doing** wrong .
- **Colour green anyone who is doing** right .

RAILWAY STATION

Do you want a fight?

Are you scared?

Now try this!

- **Talk to a partner about what the people are doing wrong.**
- **Say why it is wrong.**

**Teachers' note** Ask the children to look for people in the picture who are doing wrong. Draw out that this means doing something bad and not merely making a mistake. What could these people have chosen to do instead? Draw out that they can make choices about how to behave and that they are acting responsibly when they make the right choices.

**Developing Citizenship Year 2**
**© A & C BLACK**

# Goody bag

How can your group share the goody bag?

- Cut out the 'goodies'.
- Make it fair.

lollipop

lollipop

lollipop

lollipop

ball

puzzle

computer
game

drink

pencil

## How did you make it fair?

- Tell your teacher.

**Teachers' note** Discuss what should be done if things cannot be shared out equally among a group: for example, items left over and which cannot be shared out could be given to someone outside the group; items which can be used more than once could be used by different people at different times.

**Developing Citizenship
Year 2**
© A & C BLACK

# Pirates' shopping list

The pirates are going to sea.

- **Choose 12 healthy foods for them to pack.**
- **Write their shopping list.**

**Shopping list**

Ship's stores

| chocolate | toffee | biscuits |

| milk | butter | cheese | eggs |

| bananas | pears | lemonade |

| sugar | fish | peas | potatoes |

| cola | water | apples | cake |

| chicken | bread | doughnuts |

Now try this!

- **Tell a partner why the foods on the list are healthy.**

**Teachers' note** Ask the children what kinds of foods they think are healthy. Remind them about their previous learning and draw out that we should not eat too many foods which contain a lot of sugar or fat and that it is important to eat lots of different foods, including fruit.

**Developing Citizenship Year 2**
**© A & C BLACK**

# Give germs the boot!

**Keep germs away from food.**

• **Write four instructions.**

| | |
|---|---|
|  | _____<br>_____<br>_____ |
|  | _____<br>_____<br>_____ |
|  | _____<br>_____<br>_____ |
|  | _____<br>_____<br>_____ |

## Word bank

| clean | hands | | soap | wipe |
|---|---|---|---|---|
| cold | kitchen | spray | warm | worktop |
| fruit | rinse | | water | |

 • **Write another instruction for kicking out germs.**

**Teachers' note** Ask the children why they should wash their hands before touching food. Draw out that, in addition to dirt which can be seen, there could be harmful germs which cannot be seen on their hands. Discuss the care the children should take at school when handling and preparing food.

**Developing Citizenship**
**Year 2**
© A & C BLACK

# Magic lamp

Your wish is my command.

You can have three wishes.

They must be for very important things.

• Write your wishes on the magic lamp.

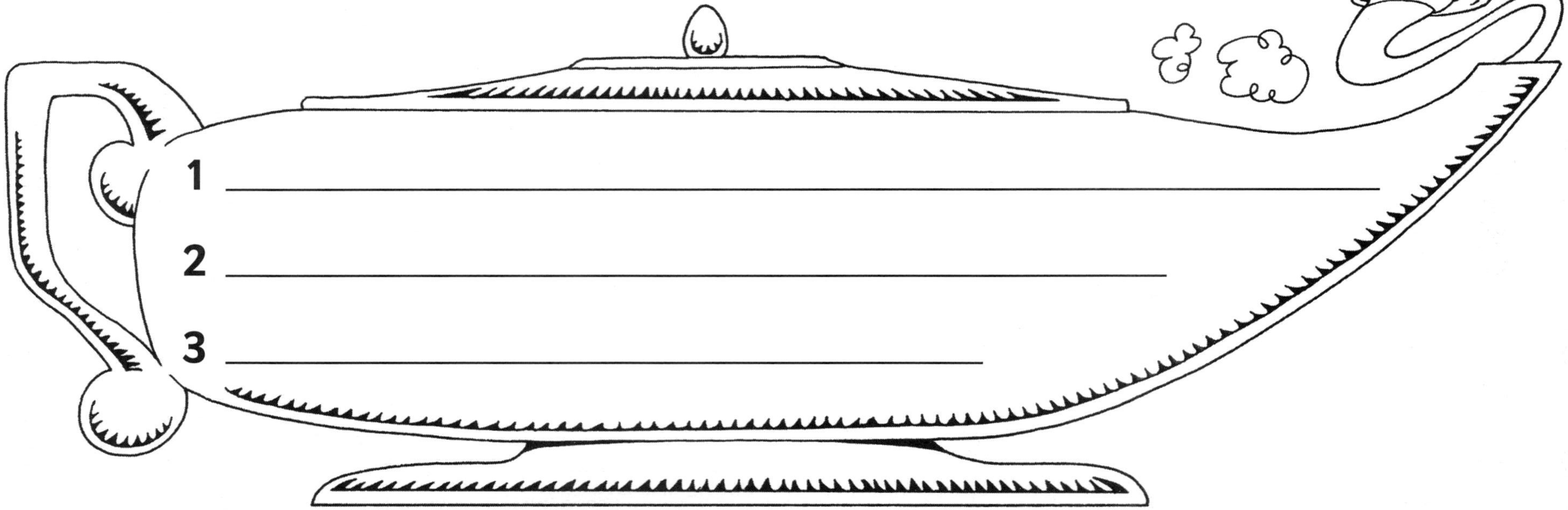

1

2

3

Why are your wishes important?

• Tell a partner.

Now try this!

**Teachers' note** Ask the children to think of three things they would ask for if they could have or do whatever they liked. Invite volunteers to talk about one of their wishes. Why is it important? Whom would it help? In what way would it make their or someone else's life better? Encourage them to think of important issues and not only material things they would like to have.

Developing Citizenship
Year 2
© A & C BLACK

# The right answer

## What should the children say?

- **Write in the speech bubbles.**

- **Tell a partner what might happen if you knocked on a door and ran away.**

**(Think about the people who live there. They might be old or ill.)**

**Teachers' note** Discuss the occasions when children do something they know is wrong because others suggest it. What stops them saying no? Draw out that many people dislike being different; they want to be like others in the group. Point out that there is nothing wrong with being different if they think they are right. Also discuss the ways in which they influence others who are younger than them. Emphasise their responsibility for setting a good example.

**Developing Citizenship**
**Year 2**
**© A & C BLACK**

# William's guinea pig

## How does Kelly feel? What will she do?

- **Draw the next picture and write a caption.**

 • **List two things Kelly did to help William. Why did she make these choices?**

**Teachers' note** Before the children begin this activity, read the book *William and the Guinea Pig* or tell them the summary of the story (see **Notes on the activities**, page 7). Have they ever asked for a pet? What did their parents or carers say? If they said yes, did they say what the children must do? If they said no, what reasons did they give? Discuss any promises the children made about looking after the pet.

**Developing Citizenship Year 2**
© **A & C BLACK**

# Copycat

## What is Callum thinking?

• **Write in the thought bubbles.**

## Why did Callum go with the others?

• **Write a sentence.**

**Teachers' note** Discuss the occasions when children do something they know is wrong because others do it. Why do they copy? What stops them saying no? Draw out that many people dislike being different; they want to be like others in the group. Point out that there is nothing wrong with being different if they think they are right.

**Developing Citizenship**
**Year 2**
© A & C BLACK

**29**

# Come and buy

## What is Sunil thinking?

- **Write in the thought bubbles.**

**Teachers' note** Ask the children about television advertisements they have seen that show items they would like to have. Do they ever ask for these things? Would thiny have asked for them if they had not seen the advertisement? Ask them about toys and other items that they already have. Do they ever see in advertisements others that they think are better?

**Developing Citizenship**
**Year 2**
**© A & C BLACK**

# Needs

## What do we all need? What for?

- **Write the words.**

**Word bank**
air
breathe
clothes
drink
eat
exercise
fit
food
home
shelter
water
wear

air to b_____

_____ to _____

_____ to _____

_____ to _____

_____ a _____ for _____

_____ to keep _____

## What do you need to be happy?

- **Write four words in the box.**

Now try this!

_____  _____

_____  _____

**Teachers' note** Discuss what is meant by *need*; it does not mean what people want, but the things they need in order to stay alive. Ask the children what else people need in order to be happy, but without which they could survive: for example, friendship and love.

**Developing Citizenship**
**Year 2**
© A & C BLACK

# Animal match: 1

- **Match the animals to the notes on pages 33 and 34.**

crow

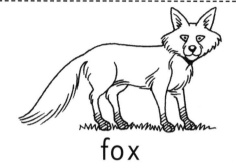
fox

greenfly

hedgehog

mouse

snail

spider

thrush

Now try this!

- **Write notes for another animal match card.**

**Teachers' note** Use this with pages 33–34. Ask the children to cut out the pictures and to work with a group to find out what each animal eats and where it lives. Discuss the meaning of 'threat' in connection with animals and ask the children about the threats faced by some animals: for example, from other animals or from people. They should also find out in what ways each animal is important (for other animals, for the environment or for people).

**Developing Citizenship**
**Year 2**
© A & C BLACK

Glue the
picture here

**Favourite foods:** grain, fruit, insects and biscuits
**Favourite places:** buildings
**Greatest fears:** cats, foxes, owls
**Why I am important:** Foxes eat me instead of killing hens.

Glue the
picture here

**Favourite foods:** slugs and insects
**Favourite places:** piles of leaves
**Greatest fears:** bonfires
**Why I am important:** I eat animals which harm garden plants and crops.

Glue the
picture here

**Favourite foods:** snails
**Favourite places:** gardens
**Greatest fears:** sparrow hawks
**Why I am important:** I eat snails and slugs, which damage plants.

Glue the
picture here

**Favourite foods:** the sap of plants
**Favourite places:** leaves
**Greatest fears:** ladybirds, other beetles, small birds and garden sprays
**Why I am important:** I am a good food for garden birds.

**Teachers' note** The children should first have cut out the animal cards on page 32. Use this with page 34. See **Notes on the activities**, page 8, for answers.

**Developing Citizenship
Year 2
© A & C BLACK**

**33**

# Animal match: 3

<table>
<tr><td>

Glue the
picture here

**Favourite foods:** flies and
other small insects
**Favourite places:** gardens and
buildings
**Greatest fears:** large birds
**Why I am important:** I eat
flies and other insect pests.

</td><td>

Glue the
picture here

**Favourite foods:** birds and
other small animals
**Favourite places:** farmland,
woods and gardens
**Greatest fears:** hunters, dogs
**Why I am important:** I get
rid of pests such as mice and
rats.

</td></tr>
<tr><td>

Glue the
picture here

**Favourite foods:** grain, berries,
insects, dead animals and
other birds' eggs
**Favourite places:** farmland
**Greatest fears:** farmers and
game-keepers
**Why I am important:** I get rid
of insects and dead animals.

</td><td>

Glue the
picture here

**Favourite foods:** living and
dead plants
**Favourite places:** gardens
**Greatest fears:** gardeners,
thrushes, slug pellets
**Why I am important:** I get
rid of dead plants in the
garden.

</td></tr>
</table>

**Teachers' note**  The children should first have cut out the animal cards on page 32. Use this with page 33. See **Notes on the activities**, page 8, for answers.

**Developing Citizenship
Year 2**
© A & C BLACK

# Wildlife garden

**FINISH**

You didn't check for hedgehogs in the bonfire. 47

46

You painted a fence with creosote. 45

44

43

37

38

39

40 You have a bird table.

41

42

36

35 You used a poisonous spray.

34

33

32

31 You have a bird box.

25

26 You have a patch of brambles.

27

28

29

30

24 You used slug pellets.

You moved a bird's nest. 23

22

21 You hang up nets of nuts for birds.

20

19

13

14

15

16

17

18 You have a boggy place for frogs.

12

11

10

9

8

7

**START**

You put a bird bath in your garden. 1

2

3

4

5 You have a rockery – slugs like it.

6

**Teachers' note** Ask the children about the animals they see in gardens at home, at school or at the homes of people they know. Draw out that insects, other small creatures (such as snails, spiders and slugs) and birds are all animals. The game is designed for four players to play like 'Snakes and ladders'.

**Developing Citizenship**
**Year 2**
© **A & C BLACK**

# On the beat

## How do police officers help?

- **Write a sentence under each picture.**

_____

_____

_____

_____

_____

_____

_____

_____

_____

_____

_____

_____

- **Draw another picture of police work.**
- **Write a caption.**

**Teachers' note** Explain the word *beat* in the context of police work. Ask the children what they have seen police officers doing (in real life and on television). How do they help people? Draw out that they protect them from others who might harm them or their property, they stop people breaking the law, they prevent accidents and they encourage safe behaviour (for example, when driving).

**Developing Citizenship**
**Year 2**
© A & C BLACK

# Missing

Tal's jumper has gone missing.

What might have happened?

• **Write in the speech bubbles.**

## Word bank

| forgot | hidden | mistake | stole |
| forgotten | left | someone | taken |
| hid | lost | somewhere | took |

• **Write what happened when something of yours went missing.**

**Teachers' note** Ask the children to think about what might have happened to Tal's jumper. After they have completed the speech bubbles, invite feedback and draw out the different reasons why things go missing (see **Notes on the activities**, page 9). Point out that one aspect of police work is looking after lost property and explain how they look after it.

**Developing Citizenship
Year 2**
© A & C BLACK

# Keep it safe

**What can you do to keep your things safe?**

- **Write three rules.**

1 _____

_____

2 _____

_____

3 _____

_____

**What should you do with lost property?**

- **Talk to your group about it.**
- **Make notes.**

**Teachers' note** Point out that, although the police and other organisations look after lost property, we have a responsibility to take care of our belongings and those of others. Ask the children what they know about how the school looks after lost property. Where is it kept? Who looks after it? Discuss what the children can do to keep their property safe.

**Developing Citizenship**
**Year 2**
**© A & C BLACK**

# Emergency call

## How should you make an emergency call?

- **Write the answers.**

① What number
should you call?

_____

② Emergency – what is
your number?

_____

③ Which service do
you need?

_____

You are connected
to that service.
They ask for your
number again, then ...

④ What is your name
and address?

Name _____

Address _____

_____

_____

_____

⑤ What has happened?

_____

_____

Now
try this!

- **Write a story about
another emergency.**

**Teachers' note** Before completing this page the children could use a disconnected telephone to enact making emergency calls for different services (ambulance, fire brigade or police – also, in places near the coast, coastguard). They could be given a badge or certificate when they have learned to recite their name, address and telephone number.

**Developing Citizenship**
**Year 2**
© A & C BLACK

# Help!

Should they call 999? ✔ or ✗

If ✔ , which service will help?

If ✗ , who can help?

- **Write in the boxes.**

You're not coming with us.

Help!

Now try this!

- **Write the story of the last picture.**
- **Give it a happy ending.**

---

**Teachers' note** It would be helpful if the children had first completed page 39. Ask them to give some examples of emergencies and to say which service(s) they would ask for in each case. If more than one service might be needed, how should they decide which to ask for first? Emphasise that if someone has (or might have been) hurt, an ambulance is the most important.

**Developing Citizenship
Year 2**
© A & C BLACK

# Hoax

## What might happen next?

- **Draw the picture and write the words.**

I'll call 999 to see what happens.

Yes – get a fire engine. We can hide and watch it.

_____

... **2 minutes later** ...

Which service do you need?

Fire brigade, please.

_____

## How could a hoax 999 call be harmful?

- **Write a story about a hoax call for an ambulance.**

Now try this!

**Teachers' note** Ask the children to discuss the first picture with a partner and to think about what the children will do next and what they will see happening. What might happen when someone else phones for a fire engine for a real fire? What could be the consequences of the children's hoax call?

**Developing Citizenship**
**Year 2**
**© A & C BLACK**

# On the safe side

## How are these children staying safe?

- **Talk to a partner about it.**

What should you do?

Now try this!

- **Write three rules for staying safe in the park.**

**Teachers' note** Ask the children about visits they have made to a park. Do the people who take them there tell them how to stay safe? What safety rules do they give them? Discuss why they give the children these rules. Write up their responses; split the rules into lists: safety from accidents and safety from people. Draw out that most people do not want to harm children but that some do.

**Developing Citizenship Year 2** © A & C BLACK

# A question of trust

Mark goes to a shop near his home.

Which people should he talk to?

- Colour them green.

Which people should he not talk to?

- Colour them red.

 How do you know when you can trust someone?

- Write three questions to ask yourself about people.

**Teachers' note** Ask the children to decide which people Mark can trust and how he knows he can trust them. You could introduce the idea of questions he asks himself: *Do I know this person? Does my mum, dad, carer (and so on) know him or her? Would my mum, dad, carer (and so on) be happy about me talking to this person? Why is he or she talking to me? What do I know about this person?*

**Developing Citizenship**
**Year 2**
© A & C BLACK

# Safety in numbers

May walks home from her gran's house.

- Follow her route: – – →.

  What should she do at each ? ?

- Talk about May's choices with a partner.

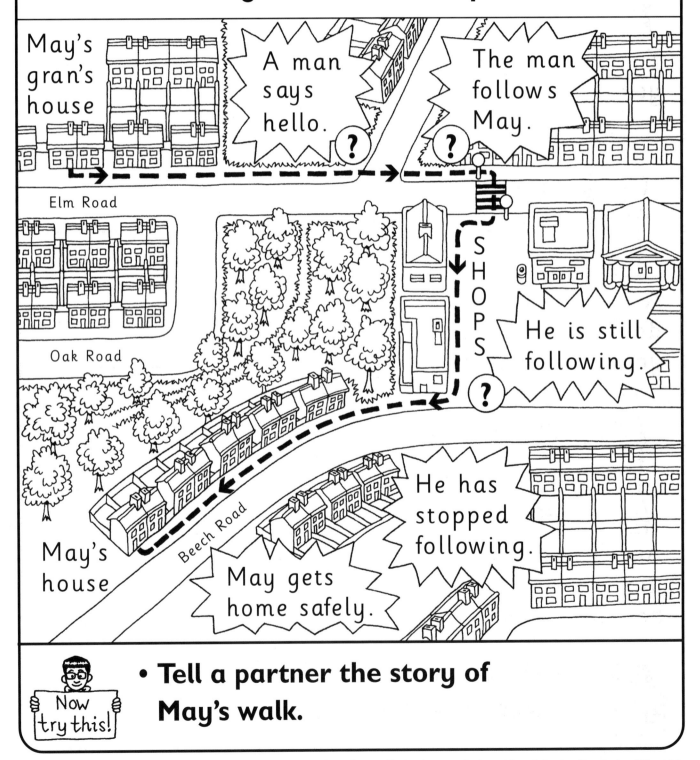

May's gran's house

Elm Road

A man says hello. ?

The man follows May. ?

Oak Road

S H O P S

He is still following. ?

May's house

Beech Road

May gets home safely.

He has stopped following.

---

**Now try this!**

- Tell a partner the story of May's walk.

---

**Teachers' note** Ask the children if they are allowed to go anywhere alone and invite them to talk about this and about how they stay safe. Do their parents or carers give them any safety rules? Write up their rules and discuss why they are important. Ask them to follow May's route on the map and to describe what she passes after she leaves her gran's house. Why does she not take a short cut through the woods?

**Developing Citizenship Year 2 © A & C BLACK**

44

## Presents

### What should you say and do?

Your auntie gives you a present.

_____

_____

_____

_____

A woman you don't know gives you some sweets.

_____

_____

_____

An older boy you don't know says he will give you £5.

_____

_____

• **Write three rules for staying safe when you are alone.**

**Teachers' note** Ask the children about presents they have been given and who gave them. Are there any presents they should not accept? Ask them to decide which presents they should accept and which they should not, and why. Invite feedback. Draw out that most presents are given for good reasons but that sometimes people offer children presents to persuade them to go somewhere with them or to do something they should not.

**Developing Citizenship**
**Year 2**
© **A & C BLACK**

# All kinds of people: 1

**Teachers' note** Ask the children to cut out the pictures on this page and on page 47, or you could laminate a set and cut it out for repeated use. Ask the children to work in a group to sort the pictures of people into sets in any way they want. Continued on page 47.

**Developing Citizenship Year 2**
© A & C BLACK

# All kinds of people: 2

**Teachers' note** Continued from page 46. Invite feedback about how the children sorted the pictures. What similarities did they use for sorting? They could have sorted them by age, disability/lack of disability, gender, race or interests.

**Developing Citizenship**
**Year 2**
© A & C BLACK

# School visitors

- Find out about visitors to your school.
- Write about them on the chart.

| Visitor's name | Where the visitor comes from | Why the visitor comes |
|---|---|---|
|  |  |  |
|  |  |  |
|  |  |  |
|  |  |  |

- Write three questions you would like to ask one of the visitors.

Teachers' note  Ask the children to name some people who come to the school apart from other children, teachers and other people who work at the school. Examples include health visitors, people who deliver mail and other items, drivers, people who collect refuse, and so on. They could carry out a survey at the main entrance of the school. Help them to find out the names of the visitors, where they come from and why they come to the school.

Developing Citizenship
Year 2
© A & C BLACK

# Interview

- **Interview a visitor to your school.**
- **Write your questions on this page.**
- **Write the visitor's answers.**

You could find out:
- why the visitor comes to your school
- how long it takes to get there
- how often the visitor comes
- what the visitor likes about the school …

| Questions | Answers |
|---|---|
| ① | ① |
| ② | ② |
| ③ | ③ |
| ④ | ④ |

Now try this!

- **Design a visitors' book for your classroom.**

You could ask the visitors to write:
- their name and address
- the date and time of their visit
- why they came.

**Teachers' note** Before the children carry out an interview, discuss what they might say to the visitor when he or she arrives. How will they greet the visitor and make him or her welcome? How will they make the visitor comfortable?

**Developing Citizenship Year 2**
© A & C BLACK

49

# Out and about

Apart from at school, where do you meet people from the local community?

- Fill in the chart for a week.

| Place | People I met |
|---|---|
|  |  |
|  |  |
|  |  |
|  |  |
|  |  |
|  |  |

- Tell a partner about the work one of these people does.

**Teachers' note** The children should first have discussed what is meant by their local community. Ask them about the places they go to near where they live. Whom do they meet there? Which people do they like to meet, and why?

**Developing Citizenship
Year 2**
© A & C BLACK

# Home sweet home

- **Write about the room where your family spends time together.**
- **Write about your partner's family's room.**

| | My family's room | My partner's family's room |
|---|---|---|
| floor | | |
| chairs | | |
| other furniture | | |
| other things | | |

**Now try this!**

- **Tell your partner about the most special thing in your room.**
- **Ask your partner about his or her most special thing.**

---

**Teachers' note** Ask the children about the room at home where their families spend most of their time together. What do they call this room? Write up their responses and discuss why we give rooms different names and why similar rooms might be given a different name by different families. Ask them about the furniture in their main family room. Draw out similarities and differences: for example, some families sit on armchairs and sofas while others prefer to sit on floor cushions or mats.

**Developing Citizenship**
**Year 2**
© A & C BLACK

# Monster train

**What is unfair on the monster train?**

• **Write on the notepad.**

## Notepad

_____

_____

_____

_____

## Could this happen in real life?

• **Talk to a partner about it.**

**Teachers' note** Ask the children to look at the picture and to describe the different carriages. Which do they think is the best? Why? Ask them if each group is being treated fairly. Why can't some monsters travel in the best carriage? Point out that this has happened to people in real life: in some countries people have not been allowed into certain places because of their nationality or the colour of their skin. Is this fair?

**Developing Citizenship**
**Year 2**
© A & C BLACK

# Fair for all

• **Write what is** fair **and** unfair **in the story.**

1  Women and girls only please.

Bus stop

_____

_____

2  £1 for adults, 50p for children.

_____

_____

3  Seat for disabled passengers

_____

_____

_____

4  You can't sit here. I don't like the look of you.

_____

_____

_____

Now try this!

• **Re-write the story.**
• **Make it fair.**

**Teachers' note** Ask the children to discuss the pictures with a partner and to decide what is going on that is not fair. They should make notes about this and note why it is not fair. When is it fair to treat people differently? Examples include different fares for adults and children and seats reserved for people with disabilities. Discuss why these are considered fair.

**Developing Citizenship Year 2**
© A & C BLACK

# Aliens all

- ## Tell the story to a partner.

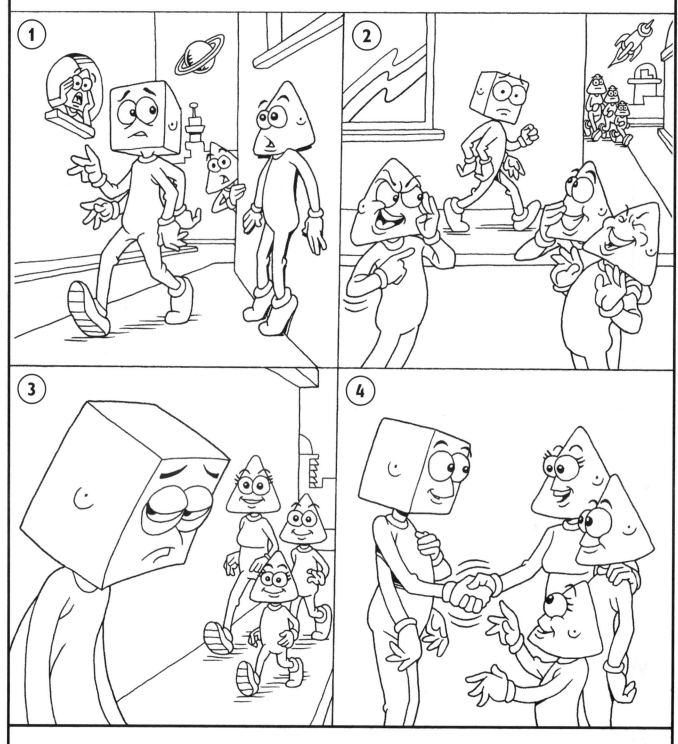

- ## Write the story.
- ## Explain why the triangle-head aliens acted as they did.

Use a computer.

**Teachers' note** After the children have read the story, ask them to re-tell it and to say why the aliens with the triangle heads were hostile to the alien with the square head. Why were they mean to him? Draw out that he was doing no one any harm and did not look as if he would harm them; they were hostile to him because he was different. Ask volunteers to share their ideas of why the family might have wanted to make friends with him.

**Developing Citizenship Year 2**
© **A & C BLACK**

# Hurting

### It Hurts

It hurts when someone makes remarks
About the clothes I wear,
About the foods I refuse to eat
Or the way I cover my hair.

It hurts when someone laughs and jokes
About the way I speak.
'Ignore them,' says my dad, but it's hard
To turn the other cheek.

It hurts when someone calls me names
Because of the colour of my skin.
Everyone's different outside
But we're all the same within.

John Foster

## How can you try to make sure that no one at your school feels like this?

- **Talk to your group.**

- **Finish the sentences.**

We can ask them to _____

_____ .

We can say _____

_____ .

If someone is teasing them we can _____

_____

_____ .

**Teachers' note** Ask the children what hurts the child in the poem. Why might others make comments about her clothes, the foods she eats or doesn't eat or about the way she covers her hair? Draw out that they might do so because these are different from what they do. What should they do instead? Discuss how they could find out more about anything which is new to them and learn to understand it. See also **Notes on the activities**, page 10.

**Developing Citizenship**
**Year 2**
© A & C BLACK

# Bullying

**What is bullying?**

• **Write in the speech bubbles.**

Bullying can be

_____

_____

_____

Bullying can be

_____

_____

_____

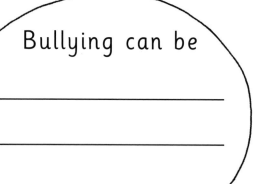

Bullying can be

_____

_____

_____

Bullying can be

_____

_____

_____

• **Write two reasons why people might bully.**

**Teachers' note** Ask the children to think about the meaning of bullying. In addition to the obvious examples, of harming someone by hitting, kicking and other physical harm, in what other ways are people bullied? Draw out that bullying includes calling names, saying hurtful things about people – anything which hurts, upsets or frightens someone on a sustained basis.

**Developing Citizenship**
**Year 2**
© A & C BLACK

# Beat the bullies

## What should they do?  or ✗

**①**
*Mop-head! Messy mop-head!*

**1a** Call the bullies names.

**b** Walk away, but tell a grown-up or a friend.

**c** Walk away and don't tell anyone.

**②**
*I told you to bring £1 for me.*

**2a** Give her the money and don't tell anyone.

**b** Give her the money but tell a grown-up.

**c** Don't give her the money and don't tell.

**d** Don't give the money but tell someone.

**③**
*We'll get you at lunchtime.*

**3a** Ask someone to stay with him.

**b** Play in a different place.

**c** Tell a teacher.

Now try this!

• **Share your answers with your group.**

**Teachers' note** Ask the children to think about what they can do if they are bullied in the ways shown in the pictures. Point out that they should not act in the same way as the bully because this kind of behaviour is wrong whoever does it. Stress the importance of telling someone; it is much easier to cope with bullying if they have help. See also **Notes on the activities**, pages 10–11.

**Developing Citizenship**
**Year 2**
© A & C BLACK

# A place to sit

## What do you like and dislike about this playground area?

| We like | We don't like |
|---|---|
| | |
| | |
| | |

**Teachers' note** The children could talk about this picture in pairs. Points to note include protection from the sun and birds, the way in which the place provides a pleasant habitat for wildlife (and how it could be improved), safety, the children's comfort and the appearance of the place (and how these could be improved).

**Developing Citizenship**
**Year 2**
© A & C BLACK

# Playground features

| | | |
|---|---|---|
| big tree | small tree | hanging basket |
| plant tub | shady bench | bench |
| bins | giant floor game | giant floor map |
| climbing frame | slide | sandpit |

**Teachers' note** Ask the children to cut out the pictures and to sort them into: features their playground has and features it doesn't have. Ask them to select the features their playground doesn't have and to sort them into: 'features we could have' and 'features we could not have'. Encourage them to give reasons why they think they could or could not have these features.

**Developing Citizenship**
**Year 2**
© A & C BLACK

# Playground survey

- **Fill in the survey about playground features.** ✔

| Feature | We have this | We do not have this | What I think of it ☺ | ☺ | ☹ |
|---|---|---|---|---|---|
| big tree | | | | | |
| small tree | | | | | |
| hanging basket | | | | | |
| plant tub | | | | | |
| shady bench | | | | | |
| bench | | | | | |
| bins | | | | | |
| giant floor game | | | | | |
| giant floor map | | | | | |
| climbing frame | | | | | |
| slide | | | | | |
| sandpit | | | | | |

- **Tell your group which one thing you would choose if you could.**
- **Say why.**

**Teachers' note** This could be used to record the children's observations of other schools' playgrounds (from visits and from photographs requested by letter or e-mail). They could use a blank copy of the chart on which to make their own list of features. Which of these features does their playground have and what do they think of the features?

**Developing Citizenship**
**Year 2**
© **A & C BLACK**

# Our choice

- **Look at pictures of other schools' playgrounds.**
- **List their features on the graph.**
- **Ask everyone to colour a box for their favourite.**

Start at the bottom.

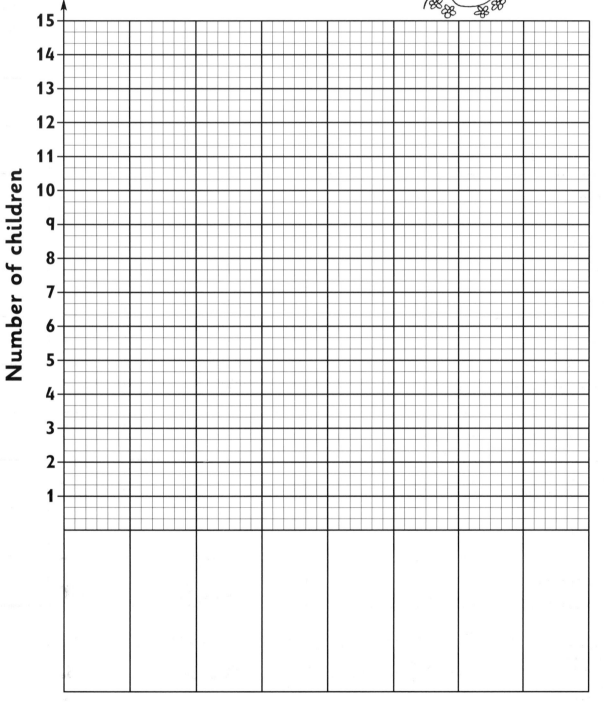

**Number of children**

15
14
13
12
11
10
9
8
7
6
5
4
3
2
1

**Features**

**Teachers' note** Use this page after the children have looked at pictures of other schools' playgrounds (these could be requested by letter or e-mail from other schools in the same country or abroad). Each group could choose up to eight features to list on the graph and then ask everyone to colour a box for their favourite. If the whole class take part, the graph could be re-numbered.

**Developing Citizenship**
**Year 2**
**© A & C BLACK**

# Finding out

## What do different children do at playtime?

- **Watch them.**
- **Ask them.**
- **Fill in the chart.**

| What they do | Age group | | |
|---|---|---|---|
| sitting games | | | |
| standing games | | | |
| ball games | | | |
| running games | | | |
| skipping games | | | |
| | | | |
| | | | |

**How suitable is the playground for what children do?**

- **Talk to a partner and make notes.**

**Teachers' note** Ask the children to think about all the different playtime activities that take place. Help them to classify them into the different types according to whether they involve mainly sitting, standing, using a ball, running, skipping or something else (what else?). Discuss for which types of activities the playground is suitable or unsuitable, and why. Could the playground be changed in any way?

**Developing Citizenship**
**Year 2**
© **A & C BLACK**

# Suggestions box

How would your group like to improve your playground?

- **Fill in forms for the** suggestions box .

Name_____

Suggestion

_____

_____

_____

_____

Name_____

Suggestion

_____

_____

_____

_____

Name_____

Suggestion

_____

_____

_____

_____

Name_____

Suggestion

_____

_____

_____

_____

Now try this!

- **Sort the suggestions with your group:** could be done **or** couldn't be done

**Teachers' note** Ask the children to think of up to four ways of improving their playground and to write them on the forms for putting in a 'suggestions box' (you could provide a special box for this purpose). After every group has completed the activity, the box could be emptied (perhaps during another lesson) and the suggestions read out and sorted according to whether or not they are feasible.

**Developing Citizenship**
**Year 2**
© **A & C BLACK**

# Agreeing and disagreeing

- **Think about this question.**

**Should ball games be allowed at playtime?**

- **Make notes about why the answer should be either** `yes` **or** `no` **.**

_because_ _____

_____

_____

_____

You might change your minds.

- **Take turns to explain your answers.**

- **Listen to one another.**

Now try this!

**What do you all think now?**

- **Vote with a tick.** ✔

|  | | | | | | Total |
|---|---|---|---|---|---|---|
| **Yes** | | | | | | |
| **No** | | | | | | |

**Teachers' note** Number the children alternately 'one' or 'two' and ask those numbered 'one' to note as many reasons as they can for allowing ball games at playtime. Ask those numbered 'two' to make notes of reasons against it. In groups of six they could argue for or against allowing ball games at playtime. Remind them that everyone should have a turn to speak and that the others should listen. After the discussion, ask them whether they have changed their minds.

**Developing Citizenship**
**Year 2**
**© A & C BLACK**